2-19-97

W9-BMU-665

PARROTS AND PARAKEETS AS PETS

A TRUE BOOK

by
Elaine Landau

Children's Press®
A Division of Grolier Publishing

New York London Hong Kong Sydney
Danbury, Connecticut

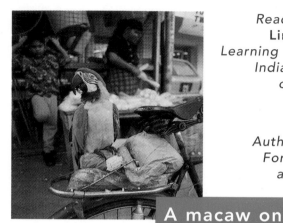

Reading Consultant
Linda Cornwell
Learning Resource Consultant
Indiana Department
of Education

Author's Dedication:
For Jerry, Bianca,
and Abraham

A macaw on
a bicycle

Visit Children's Press on the Internet at:
http://publishing.grolier.com

Library of Congress Cataloging-in-Publication Data

Landau, Elaine
    Parrots and parakeets as pets / by Elaine Landau.
        p.   cm. — (A True book)
    Includes bibliographical references and index.
    Summary: Suggests what to consider when selecting a parrot or para-
keet for a pet, and explains its housing, food, and health care needs.
    ISBN 0-516-20385-1 (lib. bdg.)   0-516-26272-6 (pbk.)
    1. Parrots—Juvenile literature. 2. Budgerigar—Juvenile literature [1.
Parrots. 2. Parakeets. 3. Pets] I. Title. II. Series.
SF473.P3L34 1997
636.6'863—dc21
                                                                97-21768
                                                                    CIP
                                                                    AC

Contents

This girl makes a great perch for these macaws.

Parrots and Parakeets

What do you think of when you picture a parrot? Do you imagine a very large bird? Is it a brightly colored bird in a far-away tropical forest? Or is it a talking bird in a cage? There are actually three hundred different types of parrots. They are found in many parts of the

Parakeets come in
many different colors.

world. Some are quite familiar to us. The budgerigar or budgie, commonly known as the parakeet, is a small member of the parrot family. You can find parakeets in most pet stores.

Birds in the parrot family have two distinct characteristics. Parrots have curved or hooked beaks. They also perch in a special way. Two toes of each foot grasp the front of a branch, while the remaining two toes grasp the back.

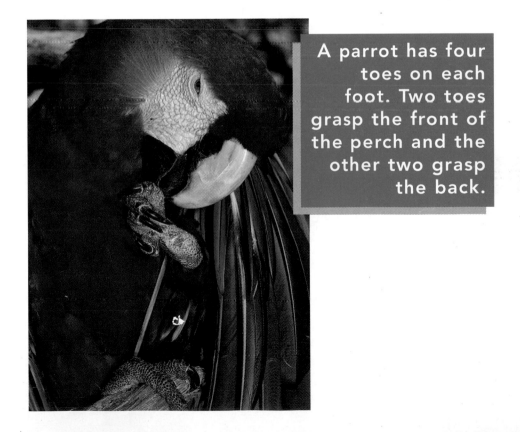

A parrot has four toes on each foot. Two toes grasp the front of the perch and the other two grasp the back.

Parrots and parakeets are extremely popular pets—and with good reason. These birds are easily tamed if handled and trained at an early age. Some parrots become extremely fond of their owners. The size of a parrot makes it an ideal pet for people who live in an apartment or a small house.

Parrots can be very entertaining, too. Many parrots mimic the human voice excellently. A talking bird can be a

Parakeets are small enough to live happily in apartments or small houses (above). Some parrots become very fond of their owners (right).

great companion and a delight to guests who did not expect to be welcomed by a bird.

9

Parakeets (above) are inexpensive and available in most pet stores. Many parrots (right) can learn to talk.

But before you buy a bird, there are some things you should keep in mind. Parakeets are inexpensive, and most pet stores sell them. But this is not so with many large parrots. Their prices vary depending on size, coloring, and availability. They can cost hundreds of dollars. A rare bird can cost thousands.

Large parrots must be carefully watched while out of their cages. Their powerful beaks can easily snap a pencil in two. They can damage furniture, and in some cases injure people. And noise can be a problem with talking parrots. In addition to talking, many of these birds have very loud and shrill natural calls. Even if the noise doesn't bother you, it may annoy your neighbors.

And be prepared to clean up after your parrot or para-keet. All pet birds create some mess. Seed husks litter the cage floor and may even land outside the cage. You'll also have to clean up bird droppings.

Think carefully before bringing home a parrot or parakeet.

Think carefully about these things before you bring a bird home. Are you willing to clean out a bird cage regularly? And if you want your parakeet or parrot to talk, do you have the time and patience to work with it? Is your family willing to help care for the bird when you can't be there?

Birds in the parrot family have long life spans. The average parakeet lives about seven or eight years, but some live into their teens and early twenties. Many large parrots are truly lifetime companions. Some have lived to be more than one hundred years old!

Larger parrots can live for a very long time.

When you buy a pet, you are making a promise to take care of it for the rest of its life. Be sure you can keep this promise before you bring a parrot or parakeet home.

Picking Out Your Bird

Most pet stores carry a wide variety of parakeets, so it won't be hard to find one. Ask the pet-store manager to show you the youngest birds. These are the easiest to tame and train to talk. Male parakeets are said to be better talkers than

Most pet stores carry a wide variety of parakeets.

females. A male parakeet
has bluish skin at its nostrils.
A female has brownish skin.

Cockatiels make gentle
and affectionate pets.

Colorful lovebirds and
cockatiels are other parrots
popular in pet stores. But
some of the larger, rarer par-

rots are harder to find. See if there is a specialty bird store in your area. If not, try to locate a parrot-breeding farm. The United States government has banned the import of these birds, so breeding farms are becoming more common.

If you can't find one in the phone book, check a bird magazine or the Internet. Bird breeders often advertise in these places.

Look for a bird
with smooth, sleek
feathers.

When buying a pet bird,
the most important thing to
look for is good health. A
healthy bird's feathers are

sleek and smooth. Beware of a bird with dull, puffed-up feathers. It's probably sick. Sick birds often sit quietly in their cages and don't seem interested in anything around them. Also, don't select a parrot that has plucked out many of its feathers.

Before making your final choice—watch the bird from a few feet away. Does it breathe smoothly and

Make sure the bird you buy breathes easily.

easily? Or is there wheezing? Check how its tail feathers move as it breathes. Breathing should look easy. If it doesn't, the bird may be ill.

Study the bird's overall behavior carefully. A healthy

bird preens itself—grooms and arranges its feathers. It appears alert and somewhat active. That's the type of pet you want.

A healthy bird preens itself.

Parrots

Some kinds of parrots, such as the scarlet macaw, hyacinth macaw, and Moluccan cockatoo, are in danger of becoming extinct in the wild. Parrot breeders raise these birds in captivity so that they can be owned as pets.

Scarlet macaw

Moluccan cockatoo

in Danger!

But sometimes breeders cannot hatch as many birds as buyers want. To make up for the lack of birds, people have illegally captured wild birds to sell. This is very harmful to the wild bird population. If you want to buy a bird that is endangered in the wild, be sure it was bred in captivity by a reliable breeder.

The baby hyacinth macaws above were bred in captivity.

Hyacinth macaw

Supplies

Before you bring home your new pet, you will need some supplies. Although some items will vary depending on the kind of parrot you pick, the items discussed here will help you get started. Ask your pet-store manager or breeder to help you with specific needs.

When buying a parrot or parakeet cage, think big. This is especially important if you leave your bird alone much of the day while you are at school. Even a small bird, such as a parakeet, needs room to exercise. A bird's cage should be at least large enough for the bird to fully spread its wings.

Stainless steel or chrome cages are best for parakeets and other small members of

A roomy stainless steel cage is good for a parakeet.

the parrot family. These cages are sturdy and never need painting. Wood or bamboo cages look nice but may be worn out by your bird's pecking. They are also difficult to clean and may attract mites and bird lice.

Cages for larger birds usually have a mesh top attached to a lower metal bottom. Sturdy wrought-iron cages also make good housing for a large parrot.

A wrought-iron cage makes a good home for a larger parrot.

Make sure the bottom of the cage has no sharp edges that might cut a parrot's foot. Also check the cage door. Parrots are extremely intelligent birds, and they often learn to open their cage door. Many owners find it safest to keep a padlock on the door.

Your bird's cage should have two or more perches. Small cages often come with plastic perches, but most bird owners prefer wooden perches. Birds

Make sure your parrot cannot open the door to its cage (left). Your bird's cage should have some wood perches (above).

like to trim their beaks by gnawing on wooden perches. Some bird owners make their own perches. Branches

Branches make great perches.

from apple trees and sycamores are great. If you use other kinds of branches, make certain that the tree is not poisonous. Also be sure that the tree hasn't been sprayed with toxic chemicals.

Toys, such as a small swing, will delight your parakeet. Pet stores usually sell a variety of bird toys. Some have bells, mirrors, and wheels for added interest. Larger toys for bigger birds are also available.

Give your parrot some toys to play with.

Feeding

It is easy to provide a healthy diet for your parakeet. Pet stores sell packaged seed mixtures especially made for them. You can buy prepared seed mixtures for other kinds of parrots too, but feed your parrot some fruits and vegetables in addition to the

seed mixture. Some bird owners also add vitamins to their
bird's food.

Attach two plastic cups—one for food and one for water—to the sides of your parakeet's cage (left). Pottery food dishes (below) are good for larger parrots.

A parakeet's cage should contain two plastic cups—one for food and the other for water. These cups attach

to the side of the cage.
However, a large bird will
destroy the plastic cups with
its powerful beak. Pottery
dishes are better for these
parrots.

You should attach a cuttlebone to a parakeet's cage. (A
cuttlebone is the shell of a
squid-like sea creature.) The
bird will sharpen and trim its
beak on it, and a cuttlebone
provides salts and minerals
birds need.

Health Care

Given a proper diet and good care, pet birds usually stay healthy. They don't come in contact with the enemies and diseases they would face in the wild.

However, caged birds can become overweight, and this can lead to health problems. Guard against this by helping your bird

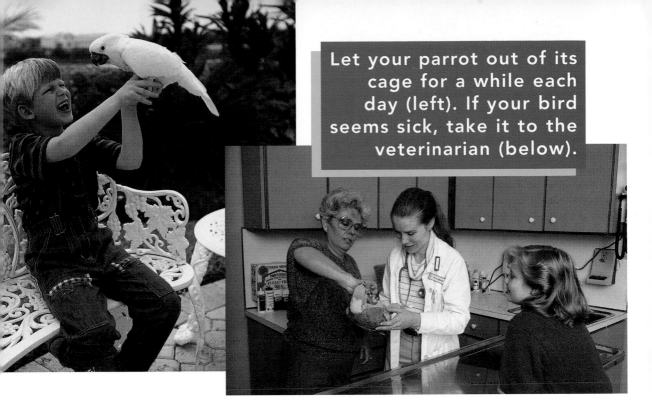

Let your parrot out of its cage for a while each day (left). If your bird seems sick, take it to the veterinarian (below).

to be active. Let it out of the cage for a while each day.

If your bird seems sick, take it to a veterinarian. Signs of illness include a loss of appetite or fluid coming from the eyes or nostrils. The bird may also be less active or seem tired or depressed.

Look Who's Talking

Animals that talk? Well, sort of. Many parrots have the ability to mimic the human voice. The best talker of all is the African grey parrot. Macaw, eclectus, and Amazon parrots are also good talkers. Some parakeets can learn to mimic speech, but they must be trained when very young. Many of the parakeets sold in pet stores are already too old to learn.

Eclectus parrots

Blue and yellow macaw

African grey parrot

You and Your Bird

Your parakeet or parrot can be a great source of fun. Once tamed, these birds will sit comfortably on your shoulder or head for long periods.

If you want a talking bird, buy only one parrot or parakeet. Two or three birds kept together will be more interested in one another than in their

A tame parrot will perch on your shoulder (left). Two parrots kept together may never learn to speak (right).

owner and may never learn to speak. Only one person should try to teach the bird to talk.

Keep repeating the word or phrase you want your bird to learn. After it learns that word, you can teach it other things. Many bird owners teach their bird its address and phone number. Such information has brought lots of lost or stolen birds back to their owners.

Put the right bird with the right person and wonderful things can happen. You may find you have a very affectionate— and talkative—new friend.

You and your pet bird will be friends for a long time.

To Find Out More

Here are some additional resources to help you learn more about parrots and parakeets:

 **Books**

Aronsky, Jim. **Crinkleroot's 25 Birds Every Child Should Know.** Bradbury Press, 1993.

Bare, Colleen Stanley. **Who Comes to the Water Hole?** Cobblehill Books, 1991.

Ganeri, Anita. **Jungle Birds.** Raintree Steck-Vaughn, 1994.

Hearne, Tina. **Parakeets.** Rourke Publications, 1989.

Hume, Rob. **Birdwatching.** Random House, 1993.

Markle, Sandra. **Outside & Inside Birds.** Bradbury Press, 1994.

Sproule, Anna. **Parakeets.** Bookwright Press, 1989.

Switzer, Merebeth. **Parrots.** Grolier, 1989.

Vrbova, Zuza. **Budgerigars.** T.F.H. Publications, 1990.

Organizations and Online Sites

Acme Pet
http://www.acmepet.com/
Includes useful information on all kinds of animals.

American Society for the Prevention of Cruelty to Animals (ASPCA)
424 East 92nd Street
New York, NY 10128-6804
(212) 876-7700, ext. 4421
http://www.aspca.org/
This organization is dedicated to the prevention of cruelty to animals. They also provide advice and services for caring for all kinds of animals.

The Aviary
http://www.theaviary.com/ci.shtml
An excellent online source of bird care information.

Pet Bird
http://www.petbird.com/
Provides information on bird care.

The Pet Bird Page
http://hookomo.aloha.net/~granty/
Descriptions and pictures of many different kinds of parrots.

Petstation
http://petstation.com/
An online service for pet owners and anyone interested in animals. Includes resources for kids.

Pet Talk
http://www.zmall.com/pet/
An online resource of animal care information.

Important Words

breeder a person who hatches birds in captivity

captivity an environment controlled by humans; not in the wild

cuttlebone the shell of a cuttlefish

endangered in danger of dying out

extinct no longer existing

mimic to copy

perch a branch, pole, or wire on which a bird rests

toxic poisonous

veterinarian a doctor who treats animals

Index

Meet the Author

Elaine Landau worked as a newspaper reporter, children's book editor, and youth services librarian before becoming a full-time writer. She has written more than ninety books for young people.

Ms. Landau lives in Florida with her husband and son.